SATURDAY NIGHT DESPERATE

from Ragged Raven Press

2003

Ragged Raven Press

Snitterfield, Warwickshire

SATURDAY NIGHT DESPERATE

First published in England, 2003 by Ragged Raven Press
I Lodge Farm, Snitterfield,
Warwickshire CV37 0LR
email: raggedravenpress@aol.com

website: www.raggedraven.co.uk

Saturday Night Desperate
ISBN 0 9542397 2 5

Set in Arial.

Printed by Lithocraft, 35a Dane Road, Coventry, West Midlands CV2 4JR

SATURDAY NIGHT
DESPERATE

The fifth anthology of poems
from Ragged Raven Press

2003

CONTENTS

FOREWORD

Ragged Raven Press was the result of a madcap idea hatched in 1998 in the Ragged Raven Hotel in Much Wenlock - the side of which you can see while John Cleese is bashing hell out of two phone boxes in *Clockwise*. Four-and-a-bit self-supporting years on and we're still here, and enjoying every bit of it.

Welcome to *Saturday Night Desperate* – poetry anthology no.5. Like its predecessors, it contains the work of invited poets and of those who entered our annual competition. The winner this year was Jamie Walsh, who at the time was working in Thailand. Runners-up were Janet Hewson, Anthony Coleman, Terence Brick and Jim Carruth.

In June we'll be releasing *Vanishing Point*, a collection by Tony Petch, examples of whose work you can find here and in some of our previous anthologies. As a parallel project we are also now editing poetry quarterly *iota*, following 17 years of sterling work by David Holliday.

In the past year Ragged Raven has taken part in the Ledbury Poetry Festival, the Purple Patch Convention in Birmingham and the Humber Mouth Literary Festival in Hull.

To find out more about Ragged Raven Press or *iota*, please look on our websites: www.raggedraven.co.uk and www.iotapoetry.co.uk or write to us at raggedravenpress@aol.com or 1 Lodge Farm, Snitterfield, Stratford-on-Avon, Warwickshire.

Bob Mee, Janet Murch

If you like *Saturday Night Desperate*, why not try other poetry from Ragged Raven Press:

the cook's wedding by John Robinson £6.99 ISBN 0 9520807 8 8
people from bones by Bron Bateman & Kelly Pilgrim £6.50 ISBN 0 9542397 0 9
Red Hot Fiesta (anthology) £6 ISBN 0 9520807 7 X
Smile the weird joy (anthology) £6 ISBN 0 9520807 6 1
The promise of rest (anthology) £6 ISBN 0 9520807 9 6
Old songs getting younger (anthology) ISBN 0 9520807 5 3

JAMIE WALSH

chess/nightrain

Chess on the night train to Hanoi.
A tiny magnetic board with discs leery of nails.
Moves made for shape not function,
patterns not direction.
Hours pass in snap and drag.

It bothers me to lose at chess;
in no other game is this true.
I see chess as protection of the self,
not defeat of another. The other disagreed –
he searched me as if I were about to boil,
or holler like an alarm clock,
while I wondered how so many
wrong moves could be made in a face.

I lose and turn in; turn inward.
His girlfriend offers hopeful cards.
She teaches me a game known as Slave in Thailand.
Trashes me. On the bunk behind, he sleeps.
She looks back at him often,
returning with a smile and a shrug –
a movement as spare as a blink.
I watch her more than my hands.

Her father is a Maths teacher.
As we play into the darkness,
she talks of growing up in one of the towns we pass
and then being subtracted (her word).
She misses it, she tells me.
The fruit sellers who angle
their wares up to the passing train.
The unfinished houses built
a hand away from the train windows.
The homes that open onto the track –
the homage of the rooted to movement and direction.
The graves that sit defensively on nearby hills,

their lines too clean and their stones too dirty;
the dusty winds of paths leading nowhere,
or to a somewhere that is almost a grave;
the paddy grids and dike paths;
the dark water and white skies.
I miss not to belong, she says, *like this—*
She makes a button pout from her shirt with a thumb.
Tied onto my country like this.

The cards dim so she packs them away,
telling me I have an unpoker face.
We talk in fractures of destinations.
She is going home to see her father
and to arrange her wedding.
She points at her nose – an ending not a beginning.

I joke and tell her that I am trying to get lost,
as ever, yet the words move as a knight moves –
two steps forward, one step bent.
Lost is not the object; lost is never the object.
I want to be taken.

She climbs to her bed,
allows clothes to swallow her.
When she is bunk-tucked and dreaming,
and I am soused in the peculiar red of having betrayed myself,
my smoking throat awakes
and I light cigarette after cigarette,
wondering where in the world I am.

Lost—

Where would this place to the left be?
Elsewhere from legal moves, this yo-yo
of ton-pawn and smidgen-king, this false view
of myself as footling knight. This direction.
The dunce cap on this faff of a life –
angled up to be taken but ever declined,
the survivor of sixty-four squares,
the half-empty wood half-used, a piece too safe,
unsquandered, unmartyred, unnecessary.

Desolate move after desolate move.
I sleep between stations and smoke at stops.
My breath times itself to her dowry growls
and the binary of ties, and all seems to be back and forward,
back and forward, forever.

Glooms, of course –
typically I wake at dawn to find unhappiness mostly dead.
My board-bound dreams have piped themselves into
When I get older, losing my hair, many years—
the night's reason a mystery again,
or explicable only as the move from a black to a white square.

In the morning, she opens her bag,
setting out French bread and Vietnamese sausage.
We eat, open the set and play draughts,
incorporating our crumbs into the game.
I try to tell her about William Steinitz,
who once publicly challenged God to a game of chess,
offering a one pawn handicap,
but it is language too far and she does not understand.
Or perhaps she does –
You not lose good at chess, she says.

I laugh—

In the unquiet cold of the open window
I plan journeys, directions, moves.

JAMIE WALSH

you and mr. jones

You whisper to me

and I recall my old science teacher,
Mr. Jones – seventeen feet tall,
embarrassment of gum, cowardly teeth.
He set us to make paper aeroplanes,
a competition where longest haul would win.
Preparations took a week.
Nails on paper, blade-sharp creases,
pips at the wing ends –
a romance of folds and their responses.
I ended up with a creature of no height
(there was barely room to grip the stem)
and giant oblong wings.
In test flights it had flown twenty-odd yards.
I was pleased with it.

There were many schools of thought
but all were variations on the theme
that it was all in the arm –
an ism of brawn.
One by one we stood up to the white line
(toes shouted back if they strayed too far)
and the planes flew –
arm back, front leg raised, javelin-style;
a run up to the line, the dart spat from the hand;
a quick wrist snap from the hip;
tip-toe high, paper loosed like an arrow,
hand camp at rest.

A girl threw and then blew with all her might.
A boy wanked his plane in the air,
as if this would wind his effort.
One kid span in circles before letting go
but miscalculated - his wide arrow
went to the side and spanged the window;
Mr. Jones kindly marked him in for three inches.

Another aped a fancy football throw-in –
he stepped back to the wall,
turned a perfect somersault
(two sports hall bangs, hands then feet),
landed line-legal and let fly.
He had obviously practised this
over and over again,
but not with the plane in his fist –
it crushed against the floor
and flew like a scone.

One girl's darling whipped vertical,
broke its nose on the ceiling
and tumbled behind the line;
another rebelled, flipped, got its pilot in the eye.
The class fuck-knuckle took his in two fists,
squeezed it into a ball,
placed it on the line
and booted –
it did not even pass my own, which had settled
happily in the middle distance.

Until Mr. Jones stepped up
the winner was a girl
who launched vertical to laughter
yet her tight, no-wing quarrel
chandelled,
stalled,
settled
into a glide
we all knew would last forever.
She landed two feet from the far wall
and nodded to herself, pleased.
But then Jones stumped up with a design
that looked like two school rulers –
one the fuselage, one the wing –
the spoddiest thing.
On the nose was a paper clip.
Against a class of sharp darts
his bird was flightless, extinct, spastic.

Jones put his toes on the line.
He put no effort in – no snap, no spit, no whip –
he just seemed to let go
and instead of falling, the plane rose.
It felt so slow I stopped breathing.
When it hit the far wall
it had almost reached the ceiling.
But for that wall, it would be sailing still.

Perhaps it was a lesson on aerodynamics.
Perhaps it was a lesson on adulthood.
Perhaps as a kid Jones grew a taste
for piss on fireworks and couldn't give it up.
Perhaps he'd more time on his hands than we did.

(Where was I?
Yes.)

This is how you whisper,
or maybe it is how I hear –
you say a clunky something that enters my ear
and lifts and lifts and lifts.

Chandelled refers to a very steep climb by an aeroplane - if it gets too steep,
the plane can stall.

ANTHONY COLEMAN

Messier

It seems to me that there are fewer
than there were. Perhaps, I should
have noticed sooner, but my thoughts
have been elsewhere. I have counted
them. I have made an inventory. But,
there is always an imbalance and I
count them once more. The problem is
that I can never know, exactly, how
many have detached themselves, have
broken free. Every now and then, one
falls to earth and lays smouldering
in the outback, or the steppes, or a
housing estate in the north-east.
It is shown on prime-time T.V. slotted
between the latest celebrity exposé
and sports desk.
                    So insignificant a thing.
                    I am concerned.

(Charles Messier 1730 - 1817. Catalogued galaxies and star clusters.)

JANET HEWSON

Continuance

And this is the way your day takes form.

Electric-blanket-warmed you wake
and wait
for tasks to tumble into consciousness
motivating the firing of neurones
the flexion and extension of muscle
the furrowing of your mirrored face into a frown.

And this is the way
molecules in motion
march like an army of ants
erecting an edifice
of duty and discipline,
arrangement and appointment,
a system built structure stark in the grey rain.

And this is the way
the licked honey of telephone talk
the tiny touches of tenderness
the small sweetnesses
stick this shell together
this fitted frame of form and function.

And this is the way
a quantum of hope
a slight penetration of light through cloud
sparks the molecules in motion
and somehow
the chemical messages of maintenance, continuance, persistence
survive sleep to sustain one more sunrise.

(Inspired by Anne Sexton's poem *Ringing the Bells*)

ROY WOOLLEY

Loki at School

Loki the new boy
puts a live coal into his mouth
and sings words of ash.

Walking backwards on bleeding hands
his recitation of early Norse
heals our language, makes our alphabet whole again.

Loki dances like flame
across the fields, confusing
wind and tree, the sky's lone colour.

Loki becomes a girl, a taste,
a scratch in the dark, a man, myself,
a stumbling boy hurt in the woods.

Loki writhes on the ground
under the monkey-puzzle tree –
reshaping hip and torso

he folds his arm into his mouth,
hauls himself up, somersaults into himself
like a knife thrown into the dark ...

JIM CARRUTH

Kalashnikov's mower

Later
you will boast
of the prototype
to the neighbour,
who leans over the fence
a witness,
wheel it from the shed
point out the features
of note:
drive shaft
half pulley
gear case
blade cover
recoil assembly,
the gas return tube
above the barrel
a long box magazine
handle like a trigger
all made from materials
just lying around.
It is amazing
what you can do
when you put your mind
to it.
You comment
on its ruthless
accuracy,
rounds per minute,
but not the flutter felt
as you flicked
off the catch.
Pulse and rhythm
became you
breathing in
first the machine,
with time

the reek of cut grass.
The fallen,
mown down
in swathes,
evidence of its power.

(I would have preferred to invent something which helps people. A lawn mower for example - Mikhail Kalashnikov (82), inventor of the rifle named after him.)

TERENCE BRICK

The Lute-Maker of Bruges

My task is a labour
of love without romance.
My workshop's a huddle -
worthy of Bosch -
imported wood
in a garden open to the sky.
Beechwood is gold as honey,
pine is white as flour.
I see the world in a lute.

I dream in Latin and see
in Burgundian Flanders
the geometry of music
as step by cobbled step
I interweave canals,
pull a bright flannel collar
up against the northern sea.

My wife sees the world in a pancake;
I like my woman warm,
my beer cold.

Pigeons bill and coo
on the Cloth Hall Belfry
but my wife displays
a van der Weyden quietude.

But a few well-chosen words
in Old High Dutch
or indecent Flemish
reduce her to an ample grunt
on a creaky bed.

At the end of day,
I carve a Paduan rose, & clasp
a form more perfect than any lute.

When I snuff the candle
there is a waft of beeswax in the air,
rabbit skin glue beneath my fingernails
but lemon in my love's hair.

JOCELYN SIMMS

The Cartographer's Craft

Telegraph poles orchestrate the route.
Cables tighten in the molten air: soon
it will thunder. Indoors a chorus of ants
searches out ley lines, patrols the thin
carpet-square, roams glossy floor tiles.
They want their plot, to call it Antland.

They circle the chairs you and I once
hauled to Wimbledon, now stacked against
the plaster wall of our rented summer.

We left them behind a privet hedge
in Wandsworth, to be free
to cup our plastic tea and queue.
They were cheap enough to lose.

But you'd marked the spot, tattooed
the railings, counted pavement cracks.
On our return you conjured
them triumphantly from the leaves.

The coffle of ants thickens.
Garden lilies parch, strained trumpets.
I will not pick them for our table.
Instead let me smell your hair.
Tell me again about the chairs.

MIRIAM SCOTT

Heathcliff is reincarnated as a supermarket trolley

I never existed and so now
come back anonymous
a wire cage for aspirations
on recalcitrant wheels.
Prunes, fruit cocktail, apricot halves
A shopping list clipped
above my heart
I roll past whispers
from another world
aubergine, courgettes, mangetout
while stars clash overhead
and planets turn
this great cave of captured dreams
hums with a low electric murmur
teatree washing up liquid with
antibacterial agents
and enraptured shoppers
glide like ghosts
towards their lit prizes
vision driven
radiatore, conchiglie, fusillini
and I, no longer I,
dreamily content,
impassive, tamed,
drunk on odours of
steam risen bread, forest fresh toilet block
and wild rocket salad
remember myself only so far
as to veer suddenly sideways
and ram that bloody woman's ankles.
Sorry, a voice says above me.
She doesn't mean it. That's my girl.
I get ready to do it again.

DON WINTER

Saturday night desperate

We talked about it at the time clock
while we waited to punch in,
how it must have been the moon
looking half-starved and the radiator whiskey
brought us to her those Saturday nights,
and how the dog with the bowling ball
head barked from her front porch, back legs braced
to charge, front legs braced to turn
and retreat, and how a willow wept
its long springy tears across the tarpaper roof,
and how she came hard
out that door hung from one low
hinge and was on you, smelling
of possum, with slick hair and a cunt
with whiskers stiff enough to grate cheese,
and how she pitched her head back, buttoned
those green eyes and shook out punk
birdcalls under her shower cap, and how afterwards
we took turns with her in the outhouse,
the door swung half open, the lime-scented life
of the toilet seeping through
the half-moon cut in one wall, and we nodded
each other daft, winked and said *she's all that*
and a bag of chips, or something like that,
and what we left out was the only
thing true: how she laid back when she finished
with us, yawned like some cat
curled in the last pocket
of a threadbare afternoon, the dull book
of a dead moth loose in its paws.

DON WINTER

Boarded up

The end has been
happening for years.
The warped boards
are diaries
of rain. Termites comb
years out of wood.
Sparrows, a concert of them,
suspend in the rafters.
Absence remains,
grown tall in a doorway.
Chipped plates
fill up
with the moon.
The silence
of a black telephone
waiting to ring.

DON WINTER

Working late

Slumped in a rusted folding chair,
he locks the chuck into place,
keeps count of finished pieces
on a junked chalkboard.

His burden is keeping awake,
even though the roof kicks with rain,
and the wind turns
on itself in the empty truck docks.
He remembers: last month a guy on six
fell asleep for a moment
and his hand became
a red stain on the greasy cement.

He keeps the heat off, drinks black coffee,
but each piece he bends
to lift is heavier than the last.
He lugs each one to the soup of oil,
a dull light marking a field
where rain is filling in the well
of his throat.

STEPHEN CLARKE

Coming clean
(or a poem that contains a line from Matthew Sweeney)

I have lain in the bath with **The Smell of Fish**.
Indulged beneath your favourite bubbles, I'm my own
one and only in the afternoon. I have relished
the guilt of it; while you work I'm at home

worse than naked with another man's poems
and making a meal of it. In the background
Radio 4 waits for me to tune in between pages.
On the radiator, our biggest, fluffiest towel

warms for my flesh. My hands are not wet. I've
eased myself down so as not to finger-print
Sweeney's latest - Cape have done a lovely job: I
sigh about the fold-back cover and type set;

not to mention the quality paper, praises from Ruth Padel
and Charles Simic. I have met him once, Matthew,
the poet. He was solid and discerning; casual,
the sort of bloke you'd have a pint or so with.

But bath times and singular afternoons, like poems
need to end. I aim the book at the safe and dry
top of our washing basket. It angles the edge, careens
off. I watch appalled as it teeters on the rim of the toilet.

LIZ DEAKIN

Wedding ring

Just a slip of a girl, they said.
That's all she was
when he slipped it on.
Here she lies
red face swollen.
No whitening under death's
brush.
On her huge finger
time's strangler
digs deep
till worms' work
loosens its grip.

JULIA M. WIXLER

The Chimney at Southwick

The detonation, I don't remember,
nor seeing it fold inside itself;
instead, the blast of dust
that ballooned outwards
through the afternoon,
embracing our bare skin,
dulling the sun's damage
with its own;

the dry cough behind glass
choking the last coke fumes
out of drained lungs
where malignant cells, mingling
with the mucus of industry
had bred unhindered;
the greenhouse in the back yard
where mushrooms grew

and bulbous tomatoes you had to wash
before eating, the codlings
ripe in their funeral suits,
(the trees had learnt how not to choke)
the lemon peppered paint
of window ledges, the grey-green shed
that envied white its freshness;
your neighbour's urn

tucked behind the coal bunker
in superstitious fear,
its alchemy distilling
poisons for the earth.

DAVID SWANN

A drowning off Brighton Pier

Minutes after they heard his cries – the black-haired figure
in black clothes, clinging to a girder of the pier –
he was gone, carried out to sea on a huge wave.

This I learned from a coast guard in a yellow jacket
shining his torch onto the water. It was an hour
since they'd last seen him – and the tide was turning.

See, I've woken the birds, he said, and starlings rose
on his light, from wet struts. We smiled.
The guard let go of the rail and looked at his hand.

No-one could last 10 minutes in that mess - but, still,
coast guards paced the shore with chains,
searching waves for shapes of drowning men,

their faint hopes fluttering in all our chests -
until a helicopter scowled into the chaos
and revealed in its searchlight only tyres, weed.

Later, after the beam of that great machine
had raked my face and passed into the dark, I thought
of rust on his hands as he parted from the girder.

DAVID SWANN

Icarus in the drizzle

First time on Crete, thinking of temple columns
on town halls in Lancashire; teenagers
traipsing wet streets, hands in parka pockets.

Island of one tunnel, passed in seconds,
joking about bulls, mazes – stories as far-off
and blinding as the sun, which glares from rocks

as our hire car flies west, into blue air,
and I suddenly remember Miss Sten Gun,
our Classics teacher, who, bored of verbs,

brought up *Icarus, the boy who flew too high –*
she shone as she spoke - *who disobeyed,*
at the cost of his waxen wings. And fell...

Through a mountain village, where men twist beads
and widows gather nutshells in apron folds;
where a thin brown dog watches us from one eye.

Our guide book says the fighting was bad here:
dead paras falling in their 'chutes. Reprisals
on cliff-tops, in chapels, On each bend, a shrine.

And that boy fell... a story told to warn us,
or bring us down, or something she nearly knew
and was moaning to herself - I don't know which.

But that night, we lie on warm sand, watching rocks
fall from the night, and almost understand
the sea pouring its heart out to the shore.

DAVID SWANN

Joy of the mountains

is what the Greeks meant by *oregano*,
and it's here with me now in the loose rocks
of these high slopes at Europe's southern tip,

where waves filch the mountains' pockets
and freedom forces thoughts of jail on me:
spuds piled like stones, beans hardening on plates,

and the gourmet thief, hungry for justice,
though some herbs would be a start ...
who says his coffee's ground from acorns.

The plan: to do us in on our own gas,
which happened, once – in the good old days!
He stirs his mug's black tarn, says: *By the way,*

the name for gassed air is 'mephitic' –
and stares at the place where that word will hang
and stale - knowledge going nowhere, like lists

learned by the lifer, who's burned up his time
studying Classics, who knows the Greek heroes,
yet hasn't walked in a meadow for years,

who I'm trying to forget now as I climb
into mountains' joy, hearing breezes founder
where bells flash and hooves sort coins in the scree.

TOM ARGLES

Revisiting the Pico de Los Reales

The sun has retrieved those exact
modulating wavelengths of gold,
somehow, that we once saw;
déjà vu – except
it's freezing bloody cold,
and the conifers' resinous whispers
have bristled into a roar,
and the light (look again) is lean as winter,
haunted, even bitter...

Low sun glazes over, images blur;
our wide-eyed moon is nowhere,
and I am here with another girl –

actually, it's not how it appears.
This view's hazier than ours,
as if sifted through the intervening years
or overlain with silken-textured scars:
flawed dreams and half-uncovered fears
shadowing the good days, the unsurpassed hours.

She's as young as you were, that evening
we weighed our love between the sun and the moon,
and she carries her life and her love so easily –
not dreaming that the golden air could cool,
the colours blend, shift their shades, weaken
or the shadow of the mountain draw its gloom,
slowly and surely, over everything.

PAT WATSON

Arriving in Venice

Black gondolas
moored at the quayside sway
on oily water
in the dark lagoon.
Vaporetti
ply their taxi trade
like water-beetles
back and forth between
hotel and landing-stage.
The winter sky,
heavy with the threat of snow,
seems hostile, promising
calamities before our journey's end.
Despite misgivings
we must travel on,
glimpsing through fog façades
which hint of palaces
and mirrored rooms
where lonely women pace
in a waking dream.
Did we do wrong to come?
Too late to ask.
We have been here before
and let us hope
that memory can bridge the empty years
since we first came to Venice, long ago,
young and, perhaps,
in love.

WILLIAM WOOD

Corsican Night

When the rings of cuckoos' calls
Around the mountain cease
The scops owl takes up his post
In a gnarled olive tree.
His persistent single sound a pulse
A car alarm, a bleeping lorry
That reverses through my dreams
Hole punch slicing rings of sound
In the pages of the dark.
Unstoppable dripping tap.
A single fluid tone
Swelling the air with sound
Regular as a time signal
Strikes the minutes off in hoots
Anxious no brush of silence
Should wash him from the canvas
Of this rustling night.

RUTH SMITH

The Photograph

It's hard to pick you out
beside the Big Trees.
You're pocket-sized against
those monumental trunks
that rise like heavy rockets
past the pines, clean
through the canopy.

Till now we've only seen
them in museums; planed
wood with three thousand
polished rings crossed
by a single line with dates,
events that hardly signify
among these Ancient Ones.

Sun cinnamons their bark
leaving you blanched.
As I wait for the moment
when they deepen into red,
I strain to see the branches,
trees on trees with cones
that need oven heat to seed.

You shuffle your feet on
bare mineral ground
where native fires flickered
in the underbrush, consumed
whole trees but only blacked
these hulks, japanning them
where flames streaked up their sides.

This photograph of you could be
my last one of sequoias.
They've not received a fire-tithe
in a hundred years and when

the debt's called in, there'll be
a bonfire that sets birds alight
cracks rocks and kills the giants.

FAY YOUNG

Spider Love

The space between us is spanned by a thread,
gossamer and tautly stretched, but strong,
capable of holding under pressure.
On bright days we glitter, diamond dew.
In storms we billow, threads expanding,
but find purchase on the sticky strands that bind us
in these tangled webs.

We spiral through each other's lives, concentric
to our centre, our patterns clear yet complex,
two halves of a collective mesh.
We feed on one another, suck and bite,
desire and venom in equal measure,
enfolding the other closer and closer, to drink deep
of every part.

TERRY STOTHARD

Delvers

Hastening beneath the pavement,
beneath the entrance,
beneath the escalator,
to where the metal worms dance
intertwine with time,
make covenants
with each other
sing with rhythmic calypso chants;
delvers in the subterranean
tinkering through the clay
emerging briefly
to the light of day
before diving down to complete
the journey beneath the Styx
or searching through self-esteem
to the ultimate fix
of trouncing victory with jubilant defeat.

We're only looking for the truth,
we are not out in the open, seeking
to disprove
any theory that over-grounders cling
to. We know why the metal worm
screams as it enters the light of stations
and we feel the vibrations
as refugees weep and squirm
in the offices of intense mediocrity
fuelled by the safety
of malevolent bureaucracy.
We're only seeking, fumbling
for the darkest place
where we don't have to see the pain
on the face
of drowning people when it's starting
to rain.

SIRIOL TROUP

Sheep

When I write the word *sheep*, a sheep
is what I want you to see, barely a gap
between my sheep and yours.

You'll get - a hieroglyph, woolly
but exact, long-nosed, four-legged, silly
as a ... sheep.

Instant communication, pen
to paper, paper to brain -
high-speed magic

fleeced from my top hat. This mammal, grass-
eating, singular, white as snow, is yours.
Mine's a flock

on castors, gliding in shadow
through a waist-high late-August meadow,
a scene out of Blake

or Samuel Palmer: a slow stream
of plural consciousness that roams
my psyche

sheepishly, pausing to ruminate
on the countless nuances between one bleat
and the next.

My archetypal sheep gambol
away down the lane, their bags of wool
unravelling behind

and no matter how fast I run, I can't
catch their threads, can't pen them in, can't
pin them down.

They're not interested in telepathic
intercourse, they chew up semantics
like herbivores.

They graze and shit and sleep. They don't need
words to fill out their contours - all they need is cud
and water,

sky above, a patch of earth below,
perhaps the occasional dip. You see, they *know*
what they are -

it's written all over them.

EDNA EGLINTON

Great Aunt Matilda

was not quite forgotten
but put aside
for a season,

to be brought out
at the end
wreathed in flowers

and neatly packaged
for a brief
resurrection display:

- a surprise to the generation
who had heard her name
in their parents' history

and had pictured her
dominant and everlastingly
in the past.

JANE MORETON

No Headstone

You said, *You will come won't you? Visit me,*
Stand for a moment at my grave, think of
The times we shared, the walks, the flowers, wine,
Remember laughter, tears - all this with love?
So now we walk the spaces in the grass
Asking *Was it here? or here?* It remains
Unmarked.
          Remembering how we stood that day,
Tears dammed in, backs to where the great lake stains
Stern landscapes with bright bobbing sails, and buzz
Of playground boats, we try to find the spot
To leave our daffodils, murmur *Next year*
We'll ask to see the plan, and know which plot.

VICTORIA LAWLESS

Celebration

We came dressed in our brightest colours,
wore bangles, beads, glitter and feathers.
The air was spiced with the breath of lilies.
It was what you would have wanted.

No room for hymns, the bulk of a vicar,
instead we read poems, sang personal praises.
The building skipped to your favourite DJs.
It was what you would have wanted.

When they lowered you into the ground
Nina Simone cried *Here Comes the Sun.*
Then a clatter of masks. Storms broke on faces.
It was what you would have wanted.

JEREMY DUFFIELD

The man who reads road signs

In the pub, on quiz nights,
it is his specialist subject,
their design, shape, colour, their meaning.

His home is a flat in the centre of town
from where, at weekends, he watches the streets
waken, live, play, quieten to one stray drunk.

At work he adds figures, counts money,
tallies floats and bank books,
invoices and chases bad debts.

He hates oafs who swear in public,
girls who talk loudly
and who drink from bottles in the street.

His wishes are to have a car with laser headlights
to atomize bad drivers,
and to be an invisible helicopter.

At night, in unsettled dreams,
he replays his life,
talks honestly to himself.

PAT EARNSHAW

Art in Absentia
(La Cimitière du Père-Lachaise, Paris)

In this metropolis of graves,
where flagstone paths are marked
with signs like roads,
we feel the spirit of some mighty souls
preside above the bones.
Proust, Wilde and Daudet brood
beneath the turfs where porches,
grills, incised remembrances
identify the entrances
to hidden corpses.

Colette receives under a king-sized duvet,
its marble polished to the redness
of raw liver. Nearby lies poor de Musset,
heartless now, but when alive heart-broken
by Georges Sandes shifting her restless body
on to Chopin.

Inside this reservation of the famous dead
a sense of peace, release, hangs
in suspension. Though spirits fret
for volumes never written, music
unplayed, and paintings never finished,

they feel as earthly forms dissolve and rot,
consumed by beetles, carrion worms
and maggots, immense relief that all their richness,
their intensity of passion, have escaped
imprisonment of bodies, failure of senses,
the limitations of the concrete things - canvas
and paint, the instruments of music,
all the impediments of living -
assured the abstract freedom
of their future compositions.

In January light the slender cypress lean
their scarred black trunks against
an ash-grey sky. The wind
is keen. And everywhere
paths turfs and trees climb
through this most exclusive Gothic town
where as in life each artist flaunts
his own conspicuous renown.

ROGER VICKERY

epiphany

we walked on mermaid beach today
a holiday son with his sometime dad

sing me songs about the crab
sing me songs about the crab

mister crab has long and
                              tricky
                                         nippers.
he's gonna get yuh
if yuh
                    don't wear

slippers

he shrieks

and splashes in water
reflector bright
as bill's eternal mirror shades

on a green mossy rock
known as *mister lizard*
we watch the waves scrub mister's back
and pat him as the tide goes out

i can write letters   *i can write letters*

with a shell
he carves his full supply
his holy three

m for mummy
                          b for uncle bill   he is sort of
t for teddy

i shouldn't be surprised

it's down to me

to teach him
the value
of the letter *d*.

DEREK ADAMS

The Catch

Liverpool was slowly coming closer.
A girl stood pushing her long ginger hair
from her face, when
the earring fell:
bounced
on the lapel of her leather bikers jacket,
ricocheted
out over the white painted handrail,
the wind spun it in a wide arc,
glittering
orange in the sunlight.

Three inches from the water
a seagull
caught the trinket,
leaving me still waiting
for the splash -
and thinking of those long
silences
you leave on my answer-phone.

MIKE HORWOOD

Transparency

I cannot say it shines,
this light, bruised by the violet flush
of a setting sun on grey rainclouds,
that forces its way through a dull pane,

while round my feet I've spread
across the floor a hundred images
or more from the past,
each framed in its square of blue plastic,

each lacking only the right light
to effect a certain kind of release,
the freedom that comes from knowing
that nothing is hidden.

Here they lie, numbered like the years,
like my confusion of the apparent and transparent.

KEITH HARRISON

Aunt Lucy's Shop

Trains to Croydon and beyond
thundered beneath Aunt Lucy's shop,
while she made tea for mum and me
on a tiny gas-reeking two-ringed hob.
And the fishing rods rattled in their racks
and the maggots in their two-pound jars
were dancing dead dwarves' fingers.

Peter Lorre would have been
gleefully terrified in his fish-eyed way,
particularly with the maggots. And
every time a train roared by,
the tackle shop would buckle and sway,
list and shudder, creak and groan
like a galleon in a gale.

Hair bunned up, big black hatted,
fixed with huge pearl-finial'd pins,
stocky as a tradesman, broad of beam
in wrap-around floral-printed apron,
Aunt Lucy would steer herself into a chair
as if she was taking a tiller in hand.
Then she'd reach behind the reels and fish hooks

to fish out a jar of twisted walking-
stick cough candy and offer me one.
Take two, she'd say - *one for now,*
another for Ron. Ron who? I'd say.
Why, lateron. Then she'd laugh and her chins'd
wobble, their moles bouncing like blackjacks.

Dumpling cheeked, busy as a thunderstorm.
If there was an uncle I never saw him.
Perhaps he was at home with the papers and the cat,
perhaps he'd gone to sea 'n never come back ...
perhaps not. But one thing was crystal clear,

Aunt Lucy was the only skipper here,
bustling about her lurching bridge
perched on stilts above the Southeast London line.

CLIFF FORSHAW

Zen Lazarus

Peace, peace! He is not dead, he doth not sleep -
He hath awakened from the dream of life -
[...]   - We decay
Like corpses in a charnel; fear and grief
Convulse us and consume us day by day,
And cold hopes swarm like worms within our living clay.
                        Shelley, *Adonais.*

They check in but they don't check out... Roach Motel ad.

i. On Ice.

Too cool to be freaked by thoughts of death,
they check in, chill and hang out in the freezer,
swamis who've slowed their heart-beat down to zero.
As for coming back - Don't hold your breath,

but listen as they tune in to the hum
of energy, the ambient everpresent Om
of the Second Law of Thermodynamics.
- Oh the fusion of time past and future: all its mythic

systems - seeking somehow to find
the balance of its great meta-cultural Tao
in that potent California of the mind,
called, for want of better designation, the *Here and Now.*

These hard-ons held all the money, cards and luck,
the nightwatch says, *Stiff as you like, but still not worth a fuck.*

ii. Fast.

Cryonauts kicked into warp speed,
our guys *Out There*, voyaging at a constant -196C,
the Away Team boldly gone into a cold colder than Deep Space
beamed on REMs so rapid the eye can't see.

Hold tight. Hold tight. Hold tight.
They sleep so fast we'll never catch them.
Their minds have attained the speed of light.

Rocky planets before this Aeon of biological time began,
they wait for the idea of life to hitch to them on some broken star,
kick-start their evolution once again when *Nanobots* will repair
                                        the damage done.

A brotherhood who've formed a quorum in the great Alone,
they persistently remain, obdurate as stone.
Your loved one - he is not dead, he is not gone.
Death has been reduced to the status of an option.

iii. Heat Death.

In smoggy hills outside the Valley, concrete hunkers
down; this Institute's *the* survivalist's bunker.

Slipping into first, generators whine uphill against degeneration;
radiating heat, confusion, from the cold clear spot
at this *Facility's* stainless heart.

Who says nothing lasts?
Relentless science: what's new is *Neurovitrification*.
A head chilled to -130C so fast
that it becomes like ... glass.

On Main Street, USA, a head-job's $50 grand,
full body'll set you back 125.
How long before new bodies can be grown from our heads?
How long before we can stand on our own two legs,
walk out of here alive?

iv. Zen Lazarus

One's deep frozen protein, hung upside down,
a mirror image to the abattoir;
another downloads his *Personality* to disk:
Think of me as pure information.

- As for me, I'll take my chances.
Who knows if any of us will ever make it back?
Just dump my bones, my body sack
out in the fields - I'll spill my guts to dogs and pigs - Full circle.
Can't pay for any other type of trip
for worn-out nerves, cloudy jelly, tripe - *Simply recycle:*
Let me get started back at Entry Level.

Let the bugs uninstall my software
free up this planet's whirring disk,
turn memory volatile once more.

GORDON SIMMS

Why There Are Tunnels

Theories concern quartz,
silica, flint, coal:
whatever was needed.
There were surface indicators,
and hearsay promised,
whispering maybe.

Before the first prop or lintel,
the earth barely scuffed,
one could imagine other wants –
possession, sanctuary, concealment. Burial,
the echo of stone and tomb.

Or curiosity. An idle
afternoon, fruit unripe, corn still wet.
The random violence
of a casual stone-throw,
challenge, target, score.
And a rock too heavy for retaliation.

The game is to dare, to best,
obsessional scrape and tear
at the shadow on the leaden face,
sense pounded from the embankment.
Time on their hands.
No other reason.

MARGARET EDDERSHAW

Posing

Like a murderer leaving the crime-scene,
there was no backward glance.
Did he depict my innocence as Rubenesque,
shape me geometrically,
or blur the body with accumulated dots?
I concealed the event like a birthmark,
till the hot flush of it surfaced in a dream.
Though it began coolly enough.

Miss Gough, warden of our student hostel,
a gaunt stick with a melancholy expression,
as if she kept a shark below by surface tension,
asked me to pose for her friend.
A cliché beret and seedy beard admitted us
to a smoke-fumed studio.
Slothful light whispered through tired panes
onto a film-set mess of canvases.

Over bitter coffee, reminiscences of
their French Resistance past
shone a beam within Miss Gough.
Her sharp features grew round as fruit,
sadness blended into brighter hues,
words spiralled into splashes of laughter.
Gesturing brusquely at a flimsy screen,
the painter grunted about my clothes.

Tous? stumbled my shocked tongue,
but my chaperone's smile defied refusal.
Out of sight, I shuddered like a child, afraid
suddenly to use a stranger's bathroom.
For my re-entrance, I draped coy hair
over my pale flabbiness.
The sitting lasted several lifetimes,
my surfaces burning like snow,

stomach clenched under his magnifying gaze,
eyes flickering to her impassive figure.
In the car home, silence hung like a curtain.
Neither of us referred to that day again.
Within a month Miss Gough died
of a brain tumour
and I understood the sudden satyr
behind that tragic mask.

CAROLYN GARWES

Recollection

My granddaughter is hunter-gathering.
Twigs, stones, feathers, dried worms,
anything that takes a four-year-old fancy.
My hands and pockets are full of her treasures.

Her mother, her own hands
wearily full of second child, sighs –
That is positively the last thing
that Grandma is carrying.
The small face crumples – *But I **need** that for ...*
and I am transported back instantly
on memory's magic carpet
to woody walks and ridgeway paths

where a little girl engages in barter –
If I take this one and leave that one behind ...
while I sigh in exasperation.

CAROL COIFFAIT

The White Roses in Your Vase

...have never had the winds of heaven blow on them.

The White Roses have never left rain on their leaves, the little stab and suck of greenfly, the weight of foraging birds.

The White Roses have led extremely sheltered lives, learnt two foreign languages, in hot-house conditions.

The White Roses are unaware that they are over-qualified for their job.

The White Roses are aware that they have very little scent and believe it was stolen from them at birth by a bad fairy.

The White Roses would like to attend a lot of weddings until they have learnt the marriage service off by heart.

The White Roses would love to meet some red roses and a real bee.

The White Roses that are ladies would like to have pink babies.

The White Roses that are gentlemen would like to breed Jack Russells.

The White Roses want to fly in a balloon, like that one on the calendar for June, bounce on the clouds, fall gently through to Earth, make friends with their wild kin who gave them birth.

The White Roses know nothing of Molecular Biology, the Industrial Revolution, Symbolism in Pre-Raphaelite Paintings, Hook's Law, Genetic Engineering, Astronomy or War and Peace

But they are willing to learn.

DENISE BENNETT

Iris

This catwalk flower,
lofty as a model
poses yellow-eyed
in summer rain
on thin-stemmed legs;
blue, frilled tongue
licking mouthfuls of opals.

This catwalk flower
reminds me of
that blue taffeta dance dress,
that hot, summer night
in the garden
under the laburnum -
that kiss.

DENISE BENNETT

Life Drawing

If there was a fire
this is the picture
I would rescue;
a simple, spontaneous
charcoal sketch.
A ten minute exercise
set by your tutor -

a young girl
with a swag of black hair
tied in bunches,
kneeling on a cold
studio floor,
the echo of herself rising,
standing, stepping out of her body.
She has flesh in the right places.
A supple back,
slender stemmed neck.
Such deft strokes comfort me.

I put on bright colours
to draw flames
from your trembling hands.

ANDY FLETCHER

small unseaworthy flowers

small unseaworthy flowers

it's not the ocean that's artificial

but the way we think about things

after our deaths
we come back to the window
we spent so much time looking through

the battered flowers return as well
to line the path
that leads to the sea

it's then we notice

how little we saw the first time around
how each flower has an anchor
and can't be washed away by rain

ANDY FLETCHER

sequence R

rain
drips
from
the
tall
metal
railings

I
didn't
know
I'd
never
see
you
again

rain
drips
from
the
tall
metal
railings
darkening
the
concrete
below

ANDY FLETCHER

right and wrong

what are all these ticks for?

and these crosses?

who decides what's good and bad?

is a thin leg better than a fat leg?

is dark blue better than indigo?

do you agree with Wittgenstein or with Russell?

they spent all their lives clubbing shadows and trying to run
without their feet

Ludwig and Bertrand got taken over by academics and the
academics got taken over by governments

and turned into right and wrong

but is that really how it is?

maybe it's more like when the adults are sitting round on their
sensible chairs in a garden

and one of the kids sneaks up with a hosepipe and a finger
over the end

and despite the consequences lets them have it

PETER WYTON

The Walrus Pod

Their habitat was the Union Jack club
Opposite Waterloo station, hauled-up
Convivially on outmoded chairs.

In all weathers, their blubber was tweed-sheathed,
Pockets stuffed with lozenges, pipe-cleaners.
Campaign medals were stitched onto waistcoats.

Ribbons denoted their wearer's presence
At Mons, Ypres, Jutland, the Dardanelles.
The very oldest had Boer War gongs.

Precedence was established by moustache.
The more luxuriant the face-fungus,
The closer its owner sat to the fire.

Long mornings were passed in group wheezing.
Post-prandial, there was choral snoring.
Tea followed. Then a frenzy of billiards.

Young squaddies would ask them for war stories.
They talked for 'Park Drive'. They positively
Chattered for Watney's Red Barrel or Bass.

Their recollections seemed to centre on
Comfort, or the lack of it. Dry trenches,
Wet trenches. Fresh rations. Rotten rations.

About combat, they had little to say.
Pressed for gory details, faces reddened,
Necks bulged. Bone-handled walking sticks waggled.

Youth wanted to know, but age knew better.
Age smoked youth's fags, drank youth's beer, said youth
Knew Fanny Adams about Fanny Adams.

Where are they now? Long gone, like their old haunt.
Dragged off one by one, I dare say, and clubbed,
Like most pinnipeds, by Time the Hunter.

TERRY QUINN

Maritime Museum, St. Helier

I didn't know that fathom
Came from faedm
A measure of outstretched arms
No longer than the arrow
Which had stopped me
On a hot March day
As I wandered on my own
Following signs
In a museum sort of way.
An arrow
A wordvane dipped
In terms of the sea
And its turning turned
My day around
As back to the start
And a boy again
I mixed up sand and water
And launched my boat on the pond
Pushed on buttons I shouldn't
And ran round corners to hide
Let fingers brush the rich black tar
In timbers
That shivered my soul
Made up yarns for pictures
That soon became a scene
Where a father
Taught his son the knots
And splices of his skills
Around the tree and down the hole
The rabbit tried and tried
But here,
I can't believe it,
The bowline came first time
And for a time
I felt a smile
Force 2, precipitation,

That brought me back
To the forenoon watch
And ready to run ashore
Not sure
I'd play the boy again
The hours for that have passed
But glad of a place
Where the sea's embrace
Can be measured
In outstretched arms.

HELEN HAIL

House Sale

Why shouldn't I go?
Just a country house sale.

Decades ago
only child adopts a family.
Unfair
they folded me in like
Mrs. Brompton's cake mixture.
I was absorbed.

The red brick of Herefordshire
is warmly familiar,
the chestnut trees bigger.

The car park is the paddock
by the stables
and the long dead horses
wander this place
through the summer afternoon,
swishing ethereal tails,
snorting through angelic nostrils made of white satin.

And suddenly I'm in the overgrown
kitchen garden,
enclosed secret world of cabbages and pears,
scented with thyme.
I know the way from here.

I step back.

Everything is bundled up in lots.
Is this what a family comes to,
bundled lots?

Heartstopping to see this particular room
the snug.
Wet Sunday afternoons
deciding what to do
and doing nothing with all the intensity of adolescence,
so many hours.

The bedrooms laid bare,
no secrets here
anymore
and down the back stairs
I've crept down before.

In the scullery then
I see him,
the crush that defined my childhood
and he's tinkering with old radios,
it was ever thus
but he's thickened and thinned
and I'll not lie down in his shadow again.

I leave the way I came
through the walled kitchen garden
and past the stables
taking nothing.

PAUL JEFFCUTT

Underworld

And didn't I charm them.
The board were pussycats,
we chatted over sweetmeats
then closed the deal -
just pick her up and walk right out,
no looking back.
Easy, I was on my way.

Didn't spare the horses to the border,
parked up, then into the back country.
Deep valleys and caves, drab and gloomy -
no wonder their time goes so slow.
A helluva long trek down,
I reached the barricade quite knackered
but still put on a smile.
Security sneered, checked my warrant twice,
then a goon shrugged me to the place.

Yes, there she lay, lover girl:
pale, still sleeping and so cute.
I tiptoed close and stroked her cool skin,
she gasped, two blue eyes startled alight;
I grinned, *c'mon kid, we're outa here!*
(relief jumping at my throat).

Beaming, she began to rise
but one leg still swollen, from the bite,
I had to guide her to the gate.
Dogs barked, security stamped our permit:
bye-bye clever clogs, smirked one, *don't come back.*
The route out was narrow,
winding up through ravines to the pass;
I led the way, she followed unaided.
We began chatting about home
and what we'd do on our return -
champagne, steam baths, a feast, loads of nookie -
later we got on to decorations and disputed the drapes.

Across the river, the going got steep -
all I could manage was a hollow whistle,
while she whimpered under her breath.
I wanted to stop, wheel around
and sink my head into that soft neck,
wallowing in her warm duskyness,
like an animal curled in its lair;
But no turning back;
not a glance, until over the border -
that was one tough deal.

Oor-reey!
Lashing from well behind, her howl roared past,
bounced off the hillside ahead
and smacked me in the face.
I staggered,
head wobbling like a sapling in a squall
and stopped dead.

Panting, I shouted back,
Eury honey, what's happened, are you OK?
My desperate eyes flicked from side to side,
but nothing there.
The heavy quiet swirled up,
pitched onto my back
and stuck;
my thigh, held in mid-stride,
began to shake,
stones stabbing into my shoes.

Slowly my neck began to turn,
bone grating over tendons
like a knife sawing through gristle.
Then - a huge, curdling yell.
I glimpsed the scream, from the corner of my eye,
it didn't look like her
but a squashed white stripe
that roared away like a shooting star.
Soon it became a plaintive speck,
fading into the cavernous gloom;
shivering, I gaped,

my eyes began to trickle -
I blinked,
the light was gone.

Deep waters seethed,
darkly gleaming,
ready to smother and subdue.
I jolted, the chasm swayed -
how long had I been staring into these depths?
Ahead, the rocky trail curved to the pass -
my lungs filled with rich, moist air;
it tasted soft,
like summer rain.

JAN FORTUNE-WOOD

The Witness

The moon waited,
a blank canvas,
vellum white,
the curve of a question mark
framing its smile
reflected on the black lick
of a downhill river.

Our summer skin
shivered,
still warm,
and we held each other,
shaking,
breathless with the audacity
of love,
tentative fingers
tracing the landscape
of our future.

Outside your tent
the music whirled,
oblivious,
and the moon waited.

JOHN LINDLEY

The Ghost Dogs of Hyde

The Ghost Dogs of Hyde
have a nose for all things.

You can smell their breath
on the panting night air,

detect the rub of spectral fur
against your hand in the dark,

the slobber of long tongues
at the back of your knee.

Their eyes come in two colours:
black and blacker;

their heads in two sizes:
big and bigger

but soft as fog
they turn on nothing

but a sixpence,
take the corner at a lurch,

search for one another
by the wheelie bins

amongst the flung and forgotten,
the left and the lost.

The Ghost Dogs of Hyde
are pattering down Market Street,

smelling of wet rugs
in the bus shelters.

They harmonise with the traffic's growl,
visit their local haunts,

cock an ear for an inaudible whistle,
a leg for another swift wet.

Numinous, they stand guard
over nothing in particular,

spook the sinking moon with a howl,
track their pale paw prints

from dusk's grey puddles
to dawn's grey streets.

The Ghost Dogs of Hyde
come blinking red and amber at daybreak,

cross against the lights in rush hour,
slide beneath chassis, unharmed.

They are a white spectre of light
in the blue vapour of fumes,

the bark under the bonnet,
the unidentified rattle in the boot.

They are the mist on the windscreen
that the blade won't shift,

the snagged cuff on the handbrake,
the footwell's dark stain.

They are crouched imaginings
in the dazzled mind's eye,

the fleeting speck seen
then secreted in the dark cornea.

Now they are straining at the leash.
Now they are coming to heel.

And here in the mad dog midday sun
The Ghost Dogs of Hyde,

blue as wolf's bane,
are moulting like trees in Autumn,

remembering every trick they were taught
except how to play dead.

CHARLES BENNETT

How to Make a Woman Out of Water

Move to a boathouse by a river,
the walls must be yellow: the windowsills, blue.
Sleep downstairs, with your head upstream,
wait for a dream of swimming.
When it rains all night and you lie awake
reading The Observer's Book of Water,
until you know that chapter
on whirlpools and waterspouts by heart,
listen to her whisper and giggle
as she scribbles her slippery name
over and over down the glass.
Have a bucketful of oysters in the sink
in case she's feeling peckish,
and a crate of Rainwater sherry
chilling in a cave behind the waterfall.
Recover two pebbles from the well
heat them in a fire of fir cones,
next morning, cool them with a kiss
then bind them to your wrist with rushes.
Pray to become so dry
she will enter the shape of your thirst.
Prepare to be a leaf on her surface.
Taste her arrival on the wind.

TONY PETCH

Tenpin Bowling

In my vodka-soaked cries
you can detect the noise of sizzling vegetables
and remnants of cannon-shot from the Spanish Armada.
Yes dear, you say
to try to shut me up
but I throw back my head
and open my jaws even wider.
Sound solidifies
and out of my mouth spring a snooker table
Mussolini, 5000 editions of the Daily Express
a giant ant-eater
and a signal from
Voyager II saying
the world's in cloudy beta-wave high temperature danger
and we must dance and sing our way through.
By means of natural and un-natural selection,
by means of jellyfish, coinage and furniture
we must combat those who say it's disgraceful
for Colleen to be kissed
for Man U to be thrashed by Liverpool
for the train arriving at platform nine to be smoking a pipe.
I won't be defeated.
Neither will planet earth.
We have to change what we do
and to change what we do we need to allow
Shakespeare's leopardskin handcuffs to be unlocked,
the silver Paraguayan ostrich to attend the Trooping of the
                                        Colour
and the hot-dog primrose to flower.

TONY PETCH

The Ultimate Poem

I'm writing a poem.
This one's going to be truly astonishing
brilliant.
I clear the decks
shove on loads of coffee to make a start.
At last I've something important to say.
It'll really hit the big time
this one.
This one's going to have everyone laughing and weeping.
It'll make newspaper headlines.
I'll be asked to read on radio
t.v.
It'll get translated abroad
appear on university courses
get taught in schools all over the world.
For my booklaunch
fans will queue overnight.
I'll sign every flyleaf
and after shaking my hand
they won't want to wash for a week.
I no longer care about
all the stuff I've scribbled to date.
I won't have got pissed every night
on superstrength lager
for years of drunken ramblings for nothing.
The tons of scrap paper I've filched from work
will have been worth it.
This one'll show you.
Just wait till you hear it.
I'll read it out to you
when it's done.

JUDY KENDALL

The Hyeste Thyng
(Chaucer: The Franklin's Tale, line 1479)

Lies fall softly
drifting everywhere,
off-whitish outlines
half-submerged.
I sleep late, I
don't want to wake.

Walking the path
becomes so difficult.

How can I know myself
in these conditions?
Bundled in duffle coat,
unwieldy, with all-weather boots and balaclava,
struggling against the wind,
ice, sludge, the general cold.

*

One breath
beyond the muffled
silence, and
from somewhere
comes floating
the fragrance
of a hyacinth,

light,
unexpected in the snow.

*

MICHAEL KRIESEL

Up North

Staying up at dad's
old place

pauses grow
like weeds

the mailbox
catches poems

and dandelion
seeds

I'm forty
like some

card trick
done

with coloured
leaves

MICHAEL KRIESEL

Reading Li Po

Earth that drank
the snow
1,200 years ago

still
thirsty every
spring

*

so many
leaves & men
since then

you'd think
the ground
would choke

*

time may
as well
be paper

autumn
keeps
repeating

this
red leaf

between
us

MICHAEL KRIESEL

The End

The man who is writing
the end of the world
began like this

he sat down in a chair
beside a window
closed his eyes
& waited for the steam
to finish rising from
a cup of coffee

pen & paper resting
on the window sill

darkness spreading
from behind some trees
outside the window

the trees are aquamarine

what kind of trees they are
is unimportant

what's important
is the way it's already
begun

how every night
behind his eyes
a few less stars
come out

THE POETS

JAMIE WALSH lives and writes in Devon. He is currently trying to place a first novel.

ANTHONY COLEMAN spent the 60s dabbling in oils before moving on to product design which filled the middle years. Now, having gained a TEFL qualification and a renewed interest in literature, his time is divided between verse and walking the ancient woodland which laps at the door of his Suffolk home.

JANET HEWSON grew up in north London, studied zoology at university and worked for many years in local government, in the fields of housing and I.T. Her life changed direction when, at the age of 40, she was forced to retire after contracting the chronic illness ME. She now lives in Hove on the south coast and, as well as developing her interest in creative writing, she is studying for a humanities degree with the Open University. She also enjoys playing jazz piano, gardening her tiny roof terrace, and meeting friends for cups of tea by the sea.

ROY WOOLLEY was born in Derby in 1965 and currently lives in London where he works as a computer programmer.

JIM CARRUTH has been widely published in magazines and anthologies across the UK and abroad and has just completed writing his first collection *Taste the Earth* with which he is approaching possible publishers.

TERENCE BRICK was born in London in 1942. His poems have been broadcast on local radio and have appeared in a variety of little magazines and anthologies, including PEN and Arts Council publications. He is married with two daughters and lives in West Berkshire.

JOCELYN SIMMS is a previous runner-up with Ragged Raven and has won other poetry competitions. She has recently written her first play. She runs expressive writing courses (The Writers' Block) which now operate from France via email and post. With her husband she has published six poetry pamphlets representing the work of Writers' Block members (Through the Mill publishing, proceeds to charities).

MIRIAM SCOTT is a homelessness worker, hillwalker, poet and aspiring story teller living in Leeds. Her first pamphlet (*which is very good but contains not one joke*) *Going to the Island* was published by Spout Publications in 2000. Now her first joke's been published she plans to tell quite a lot more.

DON WINTER is a prolific poet from Niles, Michigan, USA.

STEPHEN CLARKE lives in Dudley.

LIZ DEAKIN: *actor, poet, artist - in no particular order. I may find a way of combining the three; maybe not. Over the past year I have been published in many poetry magazines (including **iota**) and been successful in several competitions. Most of my poems 'come to me' while clocking up my mile at the local pool.*

JULIA M. WIXLER: *I was born in Brighton 1970. I read and write poetry 'just for pleasure' as they say and have done for as long as I can remember. I'm living in Welwyn Garden City these days, working as a database specialist for a software company. Occasionally a poem finds its way into a runner's up list or a magazine like Staple, Pulsar or Envoi.*

DAVID SWANN wasted his youth running around in sunny fields instead of learning to play snooker. He has lived in Accrington, Leamington Spa, Manchester, Tooting, Amsterdam, Morecambe, and now Brighton. His working life is also all over the place. He has reported on Accrington Stanley's football matches, cleaned toilets, worked in a warehouse, written about biscuits and winches for the planet's most boring magazines, and been writer in residence at Nottingham Prison. He now teaches English at University College, Chichester. His highest break on a full size snooker table is, currently, 12.

TOM ARGLES: fieldwork has taken him to various mountain belts in the last few years, on the flimsy pretext of geological research. A three-year lectureship in isotope geochemistry at the OU has confined him to the UK while he works out what isotope geochemistry is. Happily this also means more time at home in Buckingham with his other half and two undisciplined felines - though his research students now provide an excuse for fieldwork instead.

PAT WATSON has written prose for many years but poetry only since 1999. Born in Coventry, she now lives in Stratford-upon-Avon. Her first novel, *Yesterday's Child*, was published in September, 2002, by Merton Priory Press of Cardiff.

WILLIAM WOOD lives in Sussex and writes prose and poetry. His novel, entitled *No Time For Poetry*, is scheduled to be published in March 2003.

RUTH SMITH'S poems have appeared in several magazines and anthologies including Faber and Faber's *First Pressings*. A few years ago she won the London Writers' Poetry Prize and in 2002 the Wells Festival Poetry Prize. She used to teach English in a secondary school but now gives over her time to writing.

FAY YOUNG: *Although I've been writing poems for years, they have generally served the more personal side of my writing life. At present, most of my attention is directed at my current novel, after having completed my MA in Creative Writing at the University of Sussex. I teach creative writing to adults and struggle not to spend all of my time in front of a computer.*

TERRY STOTHARD was born in Welwyn Garden City in 1962. He started writing poetry again after a long gap about ten years ago. He has had work published in *The New Writer, Tabla, Interpreter's House* and several competition anthologies. He has won prizes in the Peterloo Poetry Competition twice and was the winner of last year's Southport Open Poetry Competition. He runs poetry taster workshops for community groups, charities and schools and also works as a creative writing tutor at a college of further education.

SIRIOL TROUP started writing poetry in December 2001 and won the Poetry Monthly Open Booklet Competition for 2002 with a selection called *Moss*.

EDNA EGLINTON lives in Devon. Her poems have been published in a wide variety of magazines and anthologies. Two recent booklets are *How are Your Spirits?* and *Forever Panto*, both from Old School Press, Bondleigh.

JANE MORETON: Living in West Bromwich, I still belong to a writers' circle in Stafford which developed years ago from a workshop at Stafford College. It gives me enormous encouragement and support. I spend some time gardening, walking, trying to do something about peace and justice issues and loneliness, and being a granny. Poetry sustains me, reading and writing.

VICTORIA LAWLESS is thirty-four and lives in Lancaster. She works with adults with learning disabilities and writes poetry between shifts. She has recently completed a part-time MA in Writing Studies and is working towards her first collection.

JEREMY DUFFIELD is a Derbyshire poet whose poems have appeared in several magazines. His latest collection *Oak Apples and Heavenly Kisses* was published in 2000 by Headland.

PAT EARNSHAW is a biology graduate and author of fifteen reference books on antique laces, who returned to her childhood passion for creative writing in 1995. She has (self-)published three poetry collections under the imprint Gorse Publications, and a book of prose-poems, *My Cat Vince*, which won first prize in the Scintilla Open Poetry Competition, 2000. Her pamphlet *The Golden Hinde* was published by Redbeck Press in March 2002. In June 2002 she was awarded a South East Arts Council grant towards future work.

ROGER VICKERY (roger7@optus.com.au) and his extraordinarily celtic skin live beside a surf beach in Sydney. Since returning to writing three years ago he has won over 20 awards for poetry and short fiction. The Ragged Raven competition is his first non-Australian competition.

DEREK ADAMS was born in Walthamstow, east London in 1957 and has lived in Essex since 1985. He is a professional photographer. He has previously had poems published in many small press magazines including *Apostrophe, Clean Sheets (USA), Moonstone, Other Poetry, Poetry Nottingham, Red Lamp, Sol, Seam, Strange Horizons* (USA), *Tears in the Fence* and *Winedark Sea* (Aus.)

MIKE HORWOOD taught English in secondary schools before leaving England to teach English overseas. He has lived in Greece and Switzerland and now lives in Finland where he teaches English and writes teaching material.

KEITH HARRISON is originally from London and now lives in south west Wales. He has been composing poetry and short stories for over 30 years. He is also a traditional story-teller and musician, and practises shamanic and Reiki healing with his partner Rosi.

GORDON SIMMS is a previous winner and runner-up with Ragged Raven, and has won various other poetry competitions. He won an Arvon prize in 1998, and has had around 70 poems published in magazines. He won a play-writing competition in 2001 and has just completed his second full-length play. He lives with his wife, Jocelyn, in France, where they rent out a riverside apartment for writers and artists.

MARGARET EDDERSHAW worked for 25 years in the UK as an actor, director and university teacher of theatre. She has published on Brecht and Stanislavsky and several of her plays have been performed at the Edinburgh Festival and in London 'fringe' theatres. In 1995 she left Britain to live in Greece and since then she has over 50 poems published in anthologies and magazines and has given readings in Athens. She has produced two collections, *Riding the Rainbow* (travel poems) and *Second Homing* (poems about Greece) and donates the total sale price (£3 for each copy) to Oxfam. The collections are available via sturgess@naf.forthnet.gr).

CAROLYN GARWES is a freelance copy editor living in Oxfordshire. She started writing again two years ago after a gap of nearly thirty years. She has already had several competition successes (first prizes awarded by Writers Bureau, Essex Poets, Burton Poets) and has had poems published in a number of small press magazines and anthologies, including Envoi, Ragged Raven's 2002 anthology and The Frogmore Papers. She would like to write poetry full of angst. However, in spite of her threat to emigrate as soon as they started arriving, many of her poems end up being about her grandchildren.

CAROL COIFFAIT is an ex-patriot Scot, a victim of long shore drift now living and working in east Yorkshire.

DENISE BENNETT is a creative writing tutor and has a Master of Arts (poetry) in this subject. Her work has appeared in various poetry magazines and her pamphlet *American Dresses* was published by Flarestack in 2000. She is currently working on her second collection.

ANDY FLETCHER was born in Halifax and now lives in Hull. He studied law but has since worked as a mould operator, farm labourer, parkie, cleaner, bus driver and, currently, part-time care co-ordinator for Social Services. His poems have appeared in various UK magazines and on the Internet.

PETER WYTON is a regular performer of his work and lives in Gloucestershire.

TERRY QUINN: *I am a medical engineer working at the Preston Acute Hospital. I started writing again on my 50th birthday in 2000 after a gap of 20 years filled with travel, career and sport. I've been lucky in having several poems published since then and hope to continue to do so. My ambition would be to have a slim (or fat) book of poetry in print.*

HELEN HAIL has lived in Gloucestershire all her life. She is a lecturer in further education and, when not engaged in literary pursuits, likes to gallop her horse through the woods.

PAUL JEFFCUTT is a member of the Queen's University Writer's Group in Northern Ireland. Over the past four years he has been active as a poet, performing his work at the Irish Writer's Centre (in Dublin), at the Belfast International Festival and at the Between the Lines Festival (in Belfast). During this period, his poetry has been published in anthologies and journals. Paul works as a researcher (on creativity in organisations) and lives amidst drumlins in the unspoilt countryside of South Down.

JAN FORTUNE-WOOD is 41 and mother to four home educated children. She read theology at Cambridge, has a PhD in feminist theology and has worked as a teacher, priest and parenting adviser. She has published several books and chapters on home education and parenting and is rediscovering her creative writing voice after a series of life changing assaults and subsequent life affirming conversion to atheism. She lives in north Wales with her husband and children, and is working on a novel on ministry, motherhood and belonging (or not).

JOHN LINDLEY lives in Congleton. Published widely in magazines and anthologies he has been a prize-winner in a number of competitions. An experienced performer, he also runs poetry workshops for writers' groups, festivals and in prisons, schools, youth clubs and day care centres, as well as for those with mental and physical disabilities. A collection of his poems *Stills from November Campaigns*, was published by Tarantula in 1998. A second collection, *Scarecrow Crimes*, was published by New Hope International in 2002.

CHARLES BENNETT was born in the north west of England and now lives in Ledbury, Herefordshire, where he works as the manager of the Ledbury Poetry Festival, one of the most inspiring events in the literary calendar. His collection *Wintergreen* was published by Headland in 2002.

TONY PETCH was born in 1942. After starting out in forestry he took up social work. He currently works at the University of Lincolnshire and Humberside in Hull. From time to time he participates in and runs writing workshops and is a member of Mutiny Writers, a group that contributes to Hull's annual literature festival. Ragged Raven publishes his collection *Vanishing Point* in June 2003.

MICHAEL KRIESEL lives alone in the Wisconsin woods and has been writing since the late 1970s. He is widely published in the American small presses, and in Britain has recently had work in *iota* and *Poetry Monthly*. Two of his more recent publications are the pamphlets *Heart's Run* by Green Bean Press (2000) and *Matter Ballet* by Musclehead (2001).

Ragged Raven's poetry publications:

People from bones by Bron Bateman and Kelly Pilgrim (2002)
£6.50 ISBN 0 9542397 0 9
This is a beautiful book which I very much enjoyed reading and I can recommend to anyone who loves poetry. **Jenny Hamlett, Poetry Monthly**
The book is the work of two poets who tackle life with wit and sympathy ...Together they have created an excellent collection and deserve a wide audience. **New Hope International**

the cook's wedding by John Robinson (2001)
£6.99 ISBN 0 9520807 8 8
I especially like the vim, the large-heartedness, the celebration of life and locality. **U. A. Fanthorpe**
A poet with immense talent, a poet at war with himself. **Voice & Verse**
Accessible, visual and rich. **The New Writer**

The promise of rest (anthology 2002) £6 ISBN 0 9520807 9 6
This is one of those anthologies where you don't look for what's good, but what is exceptional ... an excellent collection. **Purple Patch**
This is the contemporary poetry of the twenty-first century ... an intriguing showcase of real life stills and vignettes in a sparkling variety of mood, colourful imagery and colloquially attuned word and phrase.
Voice and Verse

Red Hot Fiesta (anthology 2001) £6 ISBN 0 9520807 7 X
Strong, tight and characterful. **New Hope International**
An excellent collection of poetry...Do make a point of getting a copy, it's worthwhile. **Peer Poetry International**

Smile the weird joy (anthology 2000) £6 ISBN 0 9529897 6 1
An overflowing cornucopia of all that is best in contemporary poetry... there is delight on every page. **Poetry Monthly**

Old songs getting younger (anthology 1999) £6 ISBN 09520807 5 3
Brings together an interesting mix of writers. **Connections**

Out June 2003 - Vanishing point by Tony Petch
ISBN 0 9542397 3 3